My
Daily Journey
with God

A Prayer Book for Women

Mary Carlisle Beasley

BB

Brighton Books
Nashville, TN

My
Daily Journey
with God

A Prayer Book for Women

Mary Carlisle Beasley

Printed in the United States of America
Cover Design & Page Layout: *Bart Dawson*

2 3 4 5 6 7 8 9 10 • 03 04 05 06 07 08 09 10

To Montelle Carson Hardwick

Table of Contents

Introduction

Today and every day, the dawn breaks upon a world filled with countless obligations and opportunities. Many days bring excitement and celebration; some days bring exhaustion, disappointment or sadness. Whatever the day brings—whether joy or despair—God remains steadfast, ready to travel with us every step of the way. This book serves as a gentle reminder that every step of life's journey can and should be taken with God.

Women of every generation have faced the challenges of creating life and sustaining it. But, as women of this generation, we may encounter additional obstacles that our ancestors never could have imagined. We live in a world where uncertainty and danger seem to have reached global proportions. Our daily decisions require us to make choices about raising our families, loving our neighbors, building our relationships, and caring for ourselves in a society that often sends mixed messages or sets unrealistic expectations. In such an era, we need the certainty that God provides.

This book addresses topics of profound importance to women. Each chapter contains a brief word of encouragement, Bible verses, quotations, and a prayer. As you begin each day, or as you face challenges that may occur during your day, you may consult these pages. When you do so; you will be reminded that, as you take the next step in your life's journey, God remains the ultimate traveling companion.

Abundance

Every woman knows that some days are so busy and hurried that abundance seems little more than a distant promise. But, it is not. In fact, the Bible promises that we can lead lives of spiritual and emotional abundance *when* we seek the will and the word of God.

The abundance that God promises is ours for the asking, but ask we must. Every day, we should pause long enough to say a brief word of thanksgiving, to count our blessings, and to claim the joy that God intends for our lives. When we do, we are blessed...abundantly.

I am come that they might have life, and that they might have it more abundantly.

John 10:10 KJV

Thank You, Dear Lord, for the abundant life that You have promised and provided for me. In all that I say and do, please let me share Your message of hope and encouragement with my friends, my family, and my community. Please grant me the courage, Lord, to claim all of the spiritual riches that You promise, and help me to share Your abundance with all who cross my path.

Amen

In God's faithfulness lies eternal security.

Corrie ten Boom

We have ample evidence that the Lord is able to guide. The promises cover every imaginable situation. All we need to do is to take the hand he stretches out.

Elisabeth Elliot

We were born into this world to succeed, not fail.

Henry David Thoreau

Ask and it will be given you;
seek and you will find; knock
and the door will be opened to you.
For everyone who asks receives;
he who seeks finds; and to him
who knocks, the door is opened.

Matthew 7:7-8

Acceptance

When life proceeds according to our hopes and expectations, it's easy to trust in God's master plan. But, when life takes an unexpected turn for the worse, as it does from time to time, it can be easy to become discouraged or worse.

When we experience tragedies that we do not understand or situations that we cannot change, we must learn the art of acceptance. When our prayers go seemingly unanswered, we must remember that God always hears our prayers but may answer them in ways that are different from our own hopes and expectations. When we face difficult circumstances that cannot be changed, we must learn to wait patiently for God, who works according to a divine plan and according to an ordained timetable. Whatever may come, we can be comforted: God still reigns and is with us always.

⊸Father, if it is Your will, take this cup away from Me; nevertheless not My will, but Yours, be done.

Luke 22:42 NKJV

Lord, when I am discouraged, give me hope. When I am impatient, give me peace. When I face circumstances that I cannot change, please instill in me a spirit of acceptance. In all things great and small, let me trust in You, Dear Lord, knowing that You are the Giver of life and the Giver of all things good, today and forever.

Amen

Acceptance says: True, this is my situation at the moment. I'll look unblinkingly at the reality of it. But I'll also open my hands to accept willingly whatever a loving Father sends me.

Catherine Marshall

Once the "what" is decided, the "how" always follows. We must not make the "how" an excuse for not facing and accepting the "what."

Pearl Buck

Everything has its wonders, even darkness and silence, and I learn, whatever state I may be in, therein to be content.

Helen Keller

*Whatever I have, wherever I am,
I can make it through anything
in the One who makes me who I am.*

Philippians 4:12-13 MSG

Anxiety

Are you anxious? Take your anxieties to God. Are you troubled? Take your troubles to Him. Does your world seem to be trembling beneath your feet? Seek peace from the One who cannot be moved. The same God who created the universe will give you peace if you ask Him...so ask Him.

Humble yourselves, therefore, under God's mighty hand, that he may lift you up in due time. Cast all your anxiety on him because he cares for you.

1 Peter 5:6-7

Forgive me, Dear Lord, when I am anxious. Anxiety reflects a lack of trust in Your ability to meet my every need. Help me to work, Lord, and not to be anxious. And, keep me mindful, Lord, that nothing, absolutely nothing, will happen this day that You and I cannot handle together.

Amen

Worry is a cycle of inefficient thoughts whirling around a center of fear.

Corrie ten Boom

Anxiety does not empty tomorrow of its sorrows but only empties today of its strength.

Charles Spurgeon

The moment anxious thoughts invade your mind, go to the Lord in prayer. Look first to God. Then, you will see the cause of your anxiety in a whole new light.

Kay Arthur

Do not be anxious about anything, but in everything, by prayer and petition, with thanksgiving, present your requests to God.

Philippians 4:6

19

Asking God

*W*here is God? He is as near as the air that you breathe. And, if you call upon Him, He will sustain you and protect you. Are you troubled? Take your worries to God in prayer. Are you fearful? Trust God and accept His will. Are you weary? Seek God's strength. In all things great and small, seek the healing power of God's grace. He hears your prayers, and He will answer.

☞...You do not have, because you do not ask God.

James 4:2

*L*ord... You are the giver of all things good. When I am in need, let me come to You in prayer. You know the desires of my heart, Lord. Grant them, I ask, yet not my will but Your will be done.

Amen

Any concern too small to be turned into a prayer is too small to be made into a burden.

Corrie ten Boom

When I am dealing with an all-powerful, all-knowing God, I, as a mere mortal, must offer my petitions not only with persistence but also with patience. Someday I'll know why.

Ruth Bell Graham

We are women, and my plea is let me be a woman, holy through and through, asking for nothing but what God wants to give me, receiving with both hands and with all my heart whatever that is.

Elisabeth Elliot

If you believe, you will receive whatever you ask for in prayer.

Matthew 21:22

Assertiveness

When Paul wrote Timothy, he reminded his young protégé that the God he served was a bold God and that God's spirit empowered His children. Like Timothy, we face times of uncertainty and fear in the ever-changing world in which we live. God's message is the same to us today as it was to Timothy: We can live boldly because the spirit of God resides in us. Remind yourself that no matter what occurs today, if God is with you, then you are protected.

For God did not give us a spirit of timidity, but a spirit of power, of love and of self-discipline.

2 Timothy 1:7

Lord, sometimes this world is an intimidating place. I worry about my family, my job, my health, and when I do, my worries sap my strength. Lord, fill me with Your Spirit, and let me not be timid as I face the opportunities and challenges of today. And, as I overcome whatever difficulties come my way, I give You all glory and praise.

Amen

Give me the love that leads the way, the faith that nothing can dismay, the hope no disappointments tire, the passion that will burn like fire. Let me not sink to be a clod: Make me thy fuel, flame of God.

Amy Carmichael

I wanted the deepest part of me to vibrate with that ancient yet familiar longing, that desire for something that would fill and overflow my soul.

Joni Eareckson Tada

One can never consent to creep when one feels an impulse to soar.

Helen Keller

*Never be lacking in zeal,
but keep your spiritual fervor,
serving the Lord.*

Romans 12:11

Attitude

*W*ho are the greatest among us? Are they the proud and the powerful? Hardly. The greatest among us are the humble servants who care less for their own glory and more for God's glory. If we seek greatness in God's eyes, we must forever praise God's good works, not our own.

☞Your attitude should be the same as that of Christ Jesus: Who, being in very nature God, did not consider equality with God something to be grasped, but made himself nothing, taking the very nature of a servant, being made in human likeness. And being found in appearance as a man, he humbled himself and became obedient to death— even death on a cross!

Philippians 2:5-8

*H*eavenly Father, Jesus clothed Himself with humility when He chose to leave heaven and come to earth to live and die for us, His children. Lord, Jesus is my Master and my example. Clothe me with humility, Lord, so that I might be more like Your Son.

Amen

I discovered I always have choices and sometimes it's only a choice of attitude.

Judith M. Knowlton

The greater part of our happiness or misery depends on our dispositions, and not on our circumstances.

Martha Washington

We can love Jesus in the hungry, the naked, and the destitute who are dying.... If you love, you will be willing to serve. And you will find Jesus in the distressing disguise of the poor.

Mother Teresa

He has showed you, O man, what is good. And what does the Lord require of you? To act justly and to love mercy and to walk humbly with your God.

Micah 6:8

Balance

Sometimes, amid the demands of daily life, we lose perspective. Life seems out of balance, and the pressures of everyday living seem overwhelming. What's needed is a fresh perspective, a restored sense of balance...and God. If we call upon the Lord and seek to see the world through His eyes, He will give us guidance and wisdom and perspective. When we make God's priorities our priorities, He will lead us according to His plan and according to His commandments. God's reality is the ultimate reality. May we live accordingly.

☞Love the Lord your God with all your heart and with all your soul and with all your mind.

Matthew 22:37

Lord, show me how to be ambitious in Your work. Let me strive to do Your will here on earth, and as I do, let me find contentment and balance. Let me live in the light of Your will and Your priorities for my life, and when I have done my best, Lord, give me the wisdom to place my faith and my trust in You.

Amen

Make God's will the focus of your life day by day. If you seek to please Him and Him alone, you'll find yourself satisfied with life.

Kay Arthur

Don't be overwhelmed...take it one day and one prayer at a time.

Stormie Omartian

Steep your life in God-reality, God-initiative, God-provisions. Don't worry about missing out. You'll find all your everyday human concerns will be met.

Jesus (Matthew 6:33 MSG)

You will keep in perfect peace him whose mind is steadfast, because he trusts you.

Isaiah 26:3

Blessings

God gives each of us blessings that are far too numerous to count. Our blessings include life, family, freedom, friends, talents, and possessions, for starters. And, the gifts we receive from God are multiplied when we share them with others. May we always give thanks to God for our blessings, and may we always demonstrate our gratitude by sharing them.

I will bless them and the places surrounding my hill. I will send down showers in season; there will be showers of blessing.

Ezekiel 34:26

Today, Lord, I count my many blessings, beginning with my family and my friends. You have cared for me, Lord, and I will give thanks, and I will praise You always. Today, let me share Your gifts with others, just as You first shared them with me.

Amen

Jesus intended for us to be overwhelmed by the blessings of regular days. He said it was the reason he had come: "I am come that they might have life, and that they might have it more abundantly" (John 10:10 KJV).

Gloria Gaither

When God blesses us, He expects us to use those blessings to bless the lives of others.

Mary Prince

The key to a blessed life is to have a listening heart that longs to know what the Lord is saying.

Jim Cymbala

I will make you into a great nation and I will bless you; I will make your name great, and you will be a blessing. I will bless those who bless you, and whoever curses you I will curse; and all peoples of the earth will be blessed through you.

Genesis 12:2,3

Character

Character is built slowly over a lifetime. It is the sum of every right decision, every honest word, every noble thought, and every heart-felt prayer. It is forged on the anvil of honorable work and polished by the twin virtues of generosity and humility. Character is indeed a precious thing—difficult to build but easy to tear down. Protect it always.

⌐A wife of noble character who can find? She is worth far more than rubies.

Proverbs 31:10

Lord... You are my Father in Heaven. You search my heart and know me far better than I know myself. May I be Your worthy servant, and may I live according to Your commandments. Let me be a person of integrity, Lord, and let my words and deeds be a testimony to You, today and always.

Amen

Character cannot be developed in ease and quiet. Only through experience of trial and suffering can the soul be strengthened; vision cleared; ambition inspired, and success achieved.

Helen Keller

God never called us to naïveté. He called us to integrity.... The biblical concept of integrity emphasizes mature innocence not childlike ignorance.

Beth Moore

If I take care of my character, my reputation will take care of itself.

D. L. Moody

A good name is rather to be chosen than great riches....

Proverbs 22:1 KJV

Cheerfulness

ew things in life are more sad, or, for that matter, more absurd, than a grumpy Believer. God promises us a life of abundance and joy, but He does not force His joy upon us. We must claim His joy for ourselves. And, as we journey through life, the very best day to claim God's joy is today...if not sooner!

☞...a cheerful heart fills the day with a song.

Proverbs 15:15 MSG

ord, You have given me so many reasons to celebrate. Today, let me choose an attitude of cheerfulness. Let me be joyful, Lord, quick to smile and slow to anger. And, let me share Your goodness with all whom I meet so that Your love might shine in me and through me.

Amen

When I think of God, my heart is so full of joy that the notes leap and dance as they leave my pen; and since God has given me a cheerful heart, I serve him with a cheerful spirit.

Franz Joseph Haydn

What is your focus today? Joy comes when it is Jesus first, others second...then you.

Kay Arthur

A cheerful disposition is good for your health....

Proverbs 17:22 MSG

Children

Every child is a priceless gift from the Father above. And, with the Father's gift comes immense responsibility. Wise mothers understand the critical importance of raising their children with love, with discipline, and, of course, with God.

Jesus said, "Let the little children come to me, and do not hinder them, for the kingdom of heaven belongs to such as these."

Matthew 19:14

Dear Lord, You have given me a wonderful responsibility: caring for my children. Let me love them, care for them, nurture them, teach them, and lead them to You. When I am weary, give me strength. When I am frustrated, give me patience. And, let my words and deeds always demonstrate to my children the love that I feel for them…and for You.

Amen

When Jesus put the little child in the midst of His disciples, he did not tell the little child to become like His disciples, he told the disciples to become like the little child.

Ruth Bell Graham

Our faithfulness, or lack of it, will have an overwhelming impact on the heritage of our children.

Beth Moore

A child's hand in yours—what tenderness it arouses, what power it conjures. You are instantly the very touchstone of wisdom and strength.

Marjorie Holmes

And [Jesus] said: "I tell you the truth, unless you change and become like little children, you will never enter the kingdom of heaven. Therefore, whoever humbles himself like this child is the greatest in the kingdom of heaven."

Matthew 18:3,4

Communication

Think...pause...then speak: How wise is the woman who can communicate in this fashion! But all too often, in the rush to have ourselves heard, we speak first and think next...with unfortunate results. We can encourage all who cross our path if we measure our words carefully. To do so, we must speak wisely, not impulsively. We must speak honest words of encouragement and hope, not petty words of cynicism or doubt. When we do, we will bring healing and comfort to a world that needs both.

☞May the words of my mouth and the meditation of my heart be pleasing in your sight, O LORD, my Rock and my Redeemer.

Psalm 19:14

Lord, You have warned me that I will be judged by the words I speak. And, You have commanded me to choose my words carefully so that I might be a source of encouragement and hope to all whom I meet. Keep me mindful, Lord, that I have influence on many people...make me an influence for good. And may the words that I speak today be worthy of the One who has saved me forever.

Amen

There are four ways, and only four ways, in which we have contact with the world. We are evaluated and classified by these four contacts: what we do, how we look, what we say, and how we say it.

Dale Carnegie

The real art of conversation is not only to say the right thing at the right place but to leave unsaid the wrong thing at the tempting moment.

Dorothy Nevill

Many attempts to communicate are nullified by saying too much.

Robert Greenleaf

A wise man's heart guides his mouth, and his lips promote instruction.

Proverbs 16:23

Contentment

*W*here can we find contentment? Is it a result of wealth, or power, or fame? Genuine contentment is a gift from God to those who trust in Him and follow His commandments. When God dwells at the center of our families and our lives, contentment will belong to us just as surely as we belong to God.

Keep your lives free from the love of money and be content with what you have, because God has said, "Never will I leave you; never will I forsake you."

Hebrews 13:5

*F*ather...You are my contentment. Whatever my circumstances, I find contentment when I seek Your healing hand. Let me look to You, today, Father, for the peace that You have offered me through the gift of Your Son.

Amen

Oh, what a happy soul I am, although I cannot see! I am resolved that in this world contented I will be.

Fanny Crosby

We might occasionally be able to change our circumstances, but only God can change our hearts.

Beth Moore

True contentment...is getting out of any situation all that there is in it.

G. K. Chesterton

I know what it is to be in need, and I know what it is to have plenty. I have learned the secret of being content in any and every situation, whether well fed or hungry, whether living in plenty or in want. I can do everything through him who gives me strength.

Philippians 4:12,13

Courage

When the storm clouds form overhead and we find ourselves in the dark valley of despair, our faith is stretched, sometimes to the breaking point. But God is with us, and we can be comforted. Wherever we find ourselves, whether at the top of the mountain or the depths of the valley, God is there. And, because He cares for us, we can live courageously.

☞ Be strong and courageous. Do not be afraid or terrified because of them, for the LORD your God goes with you; he will never leave you nor forsake you.

Deuteronomy 31:6

Lord, sometimes I face challenges that leave me breathless. When I am fearful, let me lean upon You. Keep me ever-mindful, Lord, that You are my God, my strength, and my shield. With You by my side, I have nothing to fear. Help me to be a grateful and courageous servant this day and every day.

Amen

Courage is the price that life exacts for granting peace. The soul that knows it not knows no release from little things.

Amelia Earhart

Courage is fear that has said its prayers.

Dorothy Bernard

I have a lot of things to prove to myself. One is that I can live my life fearlessly.

Oprah Winfrey

Be of good courage, and he shall strengthen your heart, all ye that hope in the Lord.

Psalm 31:24 KJV

Difficult Times

*F*rom time to time, all of us face difficulties, discouragement, or disappointment. When we do, God stands ready to protect us. Psalm 147 promises, "He heals the brokenhearted, and binds their wounds." (v. 3 NASB) When we are troubled, we must call upon God, and then, in His own time and according to His own plan, He will heal us.

⌐The Lord is near to all who call on him, to all who call on him in truth. He fulfills the desires of those who fear him; he hears their cry and saves them.

Psalm 145:18-19

*D*ear Heavenly Father, when I am troubled, You heal me. When I am afraid, You protect me. When I face difficulties in my life, You lift me up. You are my unending source of strength, Lord; let me turn to You when I am weak. In times of adversity, let me trust Your plan and Your will for my life. And whatever my circumstances, Lord, let me always give the thanks and the glory to You.

Amen

When the hard times of life come, we know that no matter how tragic the circumstances seem, no matter how long the spiritual drought, no matter how long and dark the days, the sun is sure to break through; the dawn will come.

Gloria Gaither

Unless we form the habit of going to the Bible in bright moments as well as in trouble, we cannot fully respond to its consolations because we lack equilibrium between light and darkness.

Helen Keller

We all go through pain and sorrow, but the presence of God, like a warm, comforting blanket, can shield us and protect us, and allow the deep inner joy to surface, even in the most devastating circumstances.

Barbara Johnson

God is our refuge and strength,
an ever-present help in trouble.

Psalm 46:1

Doing the Right Thing

*O*swald Chambers, the author of the classic devotional text My Utmost For His Highest, advised, "Never support an experience which does not have God as its source, and faith in God as its result." These words serve as a powerful reminder that we are called to walk with God and to obey His commandments. Today, and every day after that, may we be examples of righteous living to our friends and our neighbors. Then, may we reap the blessings that God has promised to all those who live according to His will and His word.

⌒He has showed you, O man, what is good. And what does the LORD require of you? To act justly and to love mercy and to walk humbly with your God.

Micah 6:8

*L*ord, this world is filled with temptations, distractions, and frustrations. When I turn my thoughts away from You and Your Word, Lord, I suffer. But when I trust in Your commandments, when I turn my thoughts, my faith, and my prayers to You, I am safe. Let me live according to Your commandments. Direct my path far from the temptations and distractions of the world. Let me discover Your will and follow it, Dear Lord, this day and always.

Amen

Those who walk in truth walk in liberty.

Beth Moore

All virtue is summed up in dealing justly.

Aristotle

Let us not be content to wait and see what will happen, but give us the determination to make the right things happen.

Peter Marshall

Happy are those who deal justly with others and always do what is right.

Psalm 106:3 NLT

Emotions

*W*e humans are spiritual, intellectual, physical and, most certainly, emotional beings. And our emotions can run from joyous ecstasy to debilitating despair. Sad emotions may be caused by many things, including disappointments, sickness, loneliness, and fatigue. When our emotions begin a downward spiral, our first and best step is to seek God's help.

The Psalmist assures that God will hear our cry, lift us from darkness, and put a new song on our lips. (40:1-3) Not only will the Lord rescue us from our sadness, He will also restore us and, in time, lead us from despair to delight.

☞...ye shall be sorrowful, but your sorrow shall be turned into joy.

John 16:20 KJV

*H*eavenly Father, You are my strength and my refuge. As I journey through this day, I know that I may encounter disappointments. When I am troubled, let me turn to You. Keep me steady, Lord, and renew a right spirit inside of me this day and forever.

Amen

No matter what we are going through, no matter how long the waiting for answers, of one thing we may be sure. God is faithful. He keeps His promises. What he starts, He finishes…including His perfect work in us.

Gloria Gaither

If your heart has grown cold, it is because you have moved away from the fire of His presence.

Beth Moore

I will give you a new heart and put a new spirit in you….

Ezekiel 36:26

Encouraging Others

*L*ife is a team sport, and all of us need occasional pats on the back from our teammates. We are called upon to spread a message of encouragement and hope to the world. The world can be a difficult place, and countless friends and family members may be troubled by the challenges of everyday life. May we become beacons of encouragement to all who cross our paths.

☞...let us consider how to stimulate one another to love and good deeds.

Hebrews 10:24 NASB

*D*ear Heavenly Father, because I am Your child, I am blessed. You have loved me eternally and cared for me faithfully. Just as You have lifted me up, Lord, let me also lift up others in a spirit of encouragement and optimism and hope. Today and every day, let me share Your healing message, to whatever extent I can, to be an encouragement to others. And, Lord, may the glory be Yours.

Amen

People, even more than things, have to be restored, renewed, revived, reclaimed and redeemed and redeemed and redeemed.

Audrey Hepburn

For every one of us that succeeds, it's because there's somebody there to show you the way out.

Oprah Winfrey

Invest in the human soul. Who knows, it might be a diamond in the rough.

Mary McLeod Bethune

A cheerful look brings joy to the heart, and good news gives health to the bones.

Proverbs 15:30

Energy

If you're a woman with too many demands and too few hours in which to meet them, you are not alone. As every woman knows, the world can be a place with too many obligations and too little time in which to complete them. But, don't fret. Instead, focus upon God and upon His love for you. Then, ask Him for the strength you need to fulfill your responsibilities. God will give you the energy to do the most important things on today's to-do list if you ask Him. So ask Him.

☞...those who hope in the LORD will renew their strength. They will soar on wings like eagles; they will run and not grow weary, they will walk and not be faint.

Isaiah 40:31

Lord, let me find my strength in You. When I am weary, give me rest. When I feel overwhelmed, let me look to You for my priorities. Let Your power be my power, Lord, and let Your way be my way, today and forever.

Amen

Love the moment and the energy of the moment will spread beyond all boundaries.

Corita Kent

The world belongs to the energetic.

Ralph Waldo Emerson

Each day, look for a kernel of excitement.

Barbara Jordan

*He said unto me, My grace
is sufficient for thee: for my strength
is made perfect in weakness.*

2 Corinthians 12:9 KJV

Faith

*H*ave you, on occasion, felt your faith in God slipping away? If so, welcome to the club. We, as mere mortals, are subject to emotions like fear, worry, and doubt. When we fall short of perfect faith, God understands us and forgives us. And, God stands ready to strengthen us, to bless us, and to renew us if we turn our doubts and fears over to Him.

↪Let us hold fast the profession of our faith without wavering; for he is faithful....

Hebrews 10:23 KJV

*D*ear God, sometimes this world can be a fearful place, full of uncertainty and doubt. In those dark moments, help me to remember that You are always near and that You can overcome any challenge. Give me faith and let me remember always that with Your love and Your power, I can live courageously and faithfully today and every day.

Amen

I pray hard, work hard, and leave the rest to God.

Florence Griffith Joyner

Yes, I have doubted; I have wandered off the path; I have been lost. But I have always re-turned...my faith has waivered but has saved me.

Helen Hayes

Trust in God. Even if you fail Him, He will never fail you.

Marie T. Freeman

Faith is our spiritual oxygen. It not only keeps us alive in God, but enables us to grow stronger....

Joyce Landorf Heatherly

We live by faith, not by sight.

2 Corinthians 5:7

Family

*Y*our most prized earthly possession is not your home, your car, or your savings account. Your most prized earthly possession is, of course, your family. Your family is a priceless gift from God. Treasure it, protect it, and dedicate it to Him. When you place God at the center of your family, He will bless you and yours forever.

⌒These should learn first of all to put their religion into practice by caring for their own family....

1 Timothy 5:4

*D*ear Lord, I am blessed to be part of the family of God where I find love and acceptance. You have also blessed me with my earthly family. May I show the same love and acceptance for my own family that You have shown for me.

Amen

It matters that we should be true to one another, be loyal to what is a family—only a little family in the great Household, but still a family, with family love alive in it and action as a living bond.

Amy Carmichael

The family is the nucleus of civilization.

Ariel & Will Durant

The family. We are a strange little band of characters trudging through life sharing diseases, toothpaste, coveting one another's desserts, hiding shampoo, borrowing money, locking each other out of rooms, loving, laughing, defending, and trying to figure out the common thread that bound us all together.

Erma Bombeck

Every kingdom divided against itself will be ruined, and every city or household divided against itself will not stand.

Matthew 12:25

Fear

*E*ven dedicated followers of the Lord may find their courage tested by the inevitable disappointments and tragedies of life. The next time you find your courage tested, remember that God is as near as your next breath, and remember that He offers salvation to His children. He is your shield and your strength. Call upon Him in your hour of need and be comforted. Whatever the size of your challenge, God is bigger.

Fear thou not; for I am with thee: be not dismayed; for I am thy God: I will strengthen thee; yea, I will help thee; yea, I will uphold thee with the right hand of my righteousness.

Isaiah 41:10 KJV

*Y*ea, though I walk through the valley of the shadow of death, I will fear no evil, for thou art with me, thy rod and staff, they comfort me. Thank You Lord, that Your perfect love casts out all fear.

Amen

Fear knocked at the door. Faith answered. No one was there.

Anonymous

Anything I've ever done that ultimately was worthwhile...initially scared me to death.

Betty Bender

Stop to look fear in the face.

Eleanor Roosevelt

The only thing we have to fear is fear itself.

Franklin D. Roosevelt

I cried out to the Lord in my suffering, and he heard me. He set me free from all my fears.

Psalm 34:6 NLT

Forgiveness

*B*ecause *we are frail, fallible, imperfect hu-*
man beings, we are quick to anger,
quick to blame, slow to forgive, and even slower to
forget. But, forgiveness is God's way, and it must be
our way, too. If there exists even one person, alive
or dead, whom you have not forgiven (and that
includes yourself), follow God's commandment and
His will for your life: forgive. Hatred and bitterness
and regret are not part of God's plan for your life.
Forgiveness is.

Judge not, and ye shall not be judged: con-
demn not, and ye shall not be condemned: forgive,
and ye shall be forgiven.

Luke 6:37 KJV

*L*ord, when *I am bitter, You can change*
my unforgiving heart. When I am slow
to forgive, Your Word reminds me that forgiveness
is Your commandment. Let me be Your obedient
servant, Lord, and let me forgive others just as You
have forgiven me.

Amen

Forgiveness is not an emotion....Forgiveness is an act of the will, and the will can function regardless of the temperature of the heart.

Corrie ten Boom

We cannot out-sin God's ability to forgive us.

Beth Moore

Life appears to me to be too short to be spent in nursing animosity or registering wrong.

Charlotte Brontë

Living life as art requires a readiness to forgive.

Maya Angelou

Praise the Lord, I tell myself, and never forget the good things he does for me. He forgives all my sins and heals all my diseases.

Psalm 103:2,3 NLT

59

Friends

*F*riend: a one-syllable word describing "a person who is attached to another by feelings of affection or personal regard," but genuine friendship is much more. When we examine the deeper meaning of friendship, so many descriptors come to mind: loyalty, kindness, understanding, forgiveness, encouragement, humor, and cheerfulness, to mention but a few. Genuine friendship should be treasured and nurtured. Today and every day, may we, as Christians, resolve to be trustworthy, encouraging, loyal friends. And, may we treasure the people in our lives who are loyal friends to us.

☞A friend loves at all times, and a brother is born for adversity.

Proverbs 17:17

*L*ord, You seek abundance and joy for me and for all Your children. One way that I can share Your joy is through the gift of friendship. Help me to be a loyal friend, Lord. Let me be ready to listen, ready to encourage, and ready to offer a helping hand. Let me be a worthy servant, Lord, and a worthy friend. And may Your love shine through me today and forever.

Amen

The best times in life are made a thousand times better when shared with a dear friend.

Luci Swindoll

Oh the comfort, the inexpressible comfort of feeling safe with a person; having neither to weigh thoughts nor measure words but to pour them all out, just as it is, chaff and grain together, knowing that a faithful hand will take and sift them, keeping what is worth keeping, and then, with the breath of kindness, blow the rest away.

Marian Evans

My friends have made the story of my life. In a thousand ways they have turned my limitations into beautiful privileges and enabled me to walk serene and happy in the shadow cast by my deprivation.

Helen Keller

Greater love has no one than this, that he lay down his life for his friends.

John 15:13

Generosity

The thread of generosity is woven—completely and inextricably—into the very fabric of the godly life. If we are to be God's disciples, we, too, must give freely of our time, our possessions, and our love. Today, may we be cheerful, generous, courageous givers. The world needs our help, and we need the spiritual rewards that will be ours when we do.

☞The good person is generous and lends lavishly….

Psalm 112:5 MSG

Lord, You have been so generous with me; let me be generous with others. Help me to be generous with my time and my possessions as I care for those in need. And, make me a humble giver, Lord, so that all the glory and the praise might be Yours.

Amen

All my experience of the world teaches me that in ninety-nine cases out of a hundred, the safe and just side of a question is the generous and merciful side.

Anna Jameson

When you cease to contribute, you begin to die.

Eleanor Roosevelt

Service is the rent you pay for room on this earth.

Shirley Chisholm

Do not withhold good from those who deserve it, when it is within your power to act.

Proverbs 3:27

Gifts

All of us have special talents, and you are no exception. But, your talent is no guarantee of success; it must be cultivated and nurtured; otherwise, it will go unused...and God's gift to you will be squandered. Today, please value the gift that God has given you, nourish it, make it grow, and share it with the world. The best way to say "Thank You" for God's gifts is to use them.

Every good gift and every perfect gift is from above, and cometh down from the Father of lights.

James 1:17 KJV

Heavenly Father, You have blessed me and my family with many gifts and talents. Let us discover them, nurture them, and use them to the glory of Your Kingdom. Let us praise You, Lord, and thank You for Your gifts, and let us give all the glory to the Giver of all things good: You.

Amen

Everyone has a talent for something.

Marian Anderson

Life is not easy for any of us. But what of that? We must have perseverance and above all confidence in ourselves. We must believe that we are gifted for something and that this thing must be attained.

Marie Curie

Since we have gifts that differ according to the grace given to us, let each exercise them accordingly: if prophecy, according to the proportion of his faith; if service, in his serving; or he who teaches, in his teaching; or he who exhorts, in his exhortation; he who gives, with liberality; he who leads, with diligence; he who shows mercy, with cheerfulness.

Romans 12:6-8 NASB

God's Love

God is a loving Father. We are His children, and we are called upon to be faithful to Him. We return our Father's love by sharing it with others. We honor our Heavenly Father by obeying His commandments and sharing His message. When we do, we are blessed...and the Father smiles.

☞The unfailing love of the Lord never ends!

Lamentations 3:22 NLT

Heavenly Father, You are love. I love You, Lord, because of Your great love for me. And, as I love You more, Lord, I am then able to love my family and friends more. Let me be Your loving servant, Heavenly Father, today and throughout eternity.

Amen

Being loved by Him whose opinion matters most gives us the security to risk loving, too, even loving ourselves.

Gloria Gaither

As God's children, we are the recipients of lavish love—a love that covers a lack of recognition this world system gives us, a love that motivates us to keep trusting even when we have no idea what God is doing.

Beth Moore

Love so amazing, so divine, demands my soul, my life, my all.

Isaac Watts

His banner over me was love.

Song of Solomon 2:4 KJV

God's Plan

*G*od has plans for your life, but He won't force you to follow His will. To the contrary, He has given you free will, the ability to make choices and decisions on your own. With the freedom to choose comes the responsibility of living with the consequences of the choices you make. Study God's word, seek the Lord in prayer, and be watchful for His signs. God intends to use you in wonderful, unexpected ways. Find God's plan for your life and follow it.

☞"For I know the plans that I have for you," declares the Lord, "plans to prosper you and not to harm you, plans to give you hope and a future. Then you will call upon me and come and pray to me, and I will listen to you."

Jeremiah 29:11-12

*L*ord, You have a plan for my life that is grander than I can imagine. Let Your purposes be my purposes. Let Your will be my will. When I am confused, give me clarity. When I am frightened, give me courage. Let me be Your faithful servant, always seeking Your guidance for my life.

Amen

God has plans—not problems—for our lives. Before she died in the concentration camp in Ravensbruck, my sister Betsie said to me, "Corrie, your whole life has been a training for the work you are doing here in prison—and for the work you will do afterward."

Corrie ten Boom

God will prove to you how good and acceptable and perfect His will is when He's got His hands on the steering wheel of your life.

Stuart & Jill Briscoe

Only God's chosen task for you will ultimately satisfy. Do not wait until it is too late to realize the privilege of serving Him in His chosen position for you.

Beth Moore

...it is God who works in you to do his will and to act according to his good purpose.

Philippians 2:13

God's Support

*L*ife can be challenging, but fear not. God loves you, and He will protect you. In times of trouble, he will comfort you; in times of sorrow, He will dry your tears. When you are troubled, or weak, or sorrowful, God is as near as your next breath. Build your life on the rock that cannot be shaken…trust in God.

☞The LORD is my strength and song, and He has become my salvation; He is my God, and I will praise Him….

Exodus 15:2

*L*ord…You have promised never to leave me or forsake me. You are always with me, protecting me and encouraging me. Whatever this day may bring, I thank You for Your love and Your strength. Let me lean upon You, Father, this day and forever.

Amen

No matter what we've been, when we are touched by God we can honestly say, "Now I'm no longer the same!"

Gloria Gaither

God wants to teach us that when we commit our lives to Him, He gives us that wonderful teacher, the Holy Spirit.

Gloria Gaither

As God perfects us, He keeps us protected from the pride that might otherwise develop by veiling to some extent our progress in our own eyes....The light of the glory of His presence shines two ways: it sheds light on the knowledge of God so that we can learn to see Him more clearly, but it also sheds light on us so that we can see our own sin more clearly.

Beth Moore

For I the Lord thy God will hold thy right hand, saying unto thee, Fear not; I will help thee.

Isaiah 41:13 KJV

God's Timing

We human beings are impatient. We know what we want, and we know exactly when we want it: NOW! But, God knows better. He has created a world that unfolds according to His own timetable, not ours. Let us be patient as we wait for God to reveal the glorious plans that He has for our lives.

☞Humble yourselves, therefore, under God's mighty hand, that he may lift you up in due time.

1 Peter 5:6

Lord... Your timing is seldom my timing, but Your timing is always right for me. You are my Father, and You have a plan for my life that is grander than I can imagine. When I am impatient, remind me that You are never early or late. You are always on time, Lord, so let me trust in You...always.

Amen

Our times are in His hands; He will avenge His elect speedily; He will make haste for our help, and not delay one hour too long.

Andrew Murray

...when we read of the great biblical leaders, we see that it was not uncommon for God to ask them to wait, not just a day or two, but for years until God was ready for them to act.

Gloria Gaither

To every thing there is a season, and a time to every purpose under the heaven.

Ecclesiastes 3:1 KJV

Golden Rule

The words of Matthew 7:12 remind us that we are commanded to treat others as we wish to be treated. This commandment is, indeed, the Golden Rule for every generation. When we weave the thread of kindness into the very fabric of our lives, we give glory to the One who gave His life for us.

☞So in everything, do to others what you would have them do to you, for this sums up the Law and the Prophets.

Matthew 7:12

Dear Lord, let me treat others as I wish to be treated. Because I expect kindness, let me be kind. Because I wish to be loved, let me be loving. Because I need forgiveness, let me be merciful. In all things, Lord, let me live by the Golden Rule.

Amen

We should behave to our friends as we would wish our friends to behave to us.

Aristotle

Do all the good you can. By all the means you can. In all the ways you can. In all the places you can. At all the times you can. To all the people you can. As long as ever you can.

John Wesley

As we have therefore opportunity, let us do good unto all men, especially unto them who are of the household of faith.

Galatians 6:10 KJV

Gratitude

As children, we are taught to say "please" and "thank you." And, as adults, we should approach God in the same way. We should offer up our needs to Him in prayer ("Please, Dear Lord...."), and we should graciously give thanks for the gifts He has given us. Let us praise God and thank Him. He is the Giver of all things good.

Therefore, since we receive a kingdom which cannot be shaken, let us show gratitude, by which we may offer to God an acceptable service with reverence and awe....

Hebrews 12:28 NASB

Dear Lord, I want my attitude to be one of gratitude. You have given me much, and I deserve so little. When I think of Your grace and goodness to me, I am humbled and thankful. Today, let me express my gratitude, Lord, not just through my words but also through my deeds, and may all the glory be Yours.

Amen

Do you know that if at birth I had been able to make one petition, it would have been that I should be born blind? Because when I get to heaven, the first face that shall ever gladden my sight will be that of my Savior!

Fanny Crosby (Blind Hymn Writer)

...God has promised that if we harvest well with the tools of thanksgiving, there will be seeds for planting in the spring.

Gloria Gaither

Each day comes bearing its own gifts. Untie the ribbons.

Ruth Ann Schabacker

I will praise the name of God with a song, and will magnify him with thanksgiving.

Psalm 69:30 KJV

Grief

*A*ll of us experience adversity and pain. When we lose something—or someone—we love, we grieve our losses. During times of heartache—or heartbreak—we can turn to God for solace. When we do, He comforts us and, in time, He heals us.

☞I have heard your prayer, I have seen your tears; behold, I will heal you....

II Kings 20:5 RSV

*Y*ou have promised, Lord, that You will not give me any more than I can bear. You have promised to lift me up out of my grief and despair. You have promised to put a new song on my lips. I thank You, Lord, for sustaining me in my day of sorrow. Restore me, and heal me, and use me as You will.

Amen

I do not believe that sheer suffering teaches. If suffering alone taught, all the world would be wise. To suffering must be added mourning, understanding, patience, love, openness and the willingness to remain vulnerable.

Anne Morrow Lindbergh

Flowers grow out of dark moments.

Corita Kent

In the final analysis, the questions of why bad things happen to good people transmutes itself into some very different questions, no longer asking why something happened, but asking how we will respond, what we intend to do now that it happened.

Harold S. Kushner

Weeping may go on all night,
but joy comes with the morning.

Psalm 30:5 NLT

Happiness

Happiness depends less upon our circumstances than upon our thoughts. When we turn our thoughts to God, to His gifts, and to His glorious creation, we experience the joy that God intends for His children. But, when we focus on the negative aspects of life, we suffer needlessly. Today and every day, let us turn our thoughts—and our hearts—to God.

Happy are those who fear the Lord. Yes, happy are those who delight in doing his commands.

Psalm 112:1 NLT

Dear Lord... You are my strength and my joy. I will rejoice in the day that You have made, and I will give thanks for the countless blessings that You have given me. Let me always be joyful, Lord, as I share Your love, and let me praise You for all the marvelous things you have done.

Amen

It is not easy to find happiness in ourselves, and it is not possible to find it elsewhere.

Agnes Repplier

If only we'd stop trying to be happy, we could have a pretty good time.

Edith Whorton

Earth's crammed with heaven.

Elizabeth Barrett Browning

This is happiness: to be dissolved in something complete and great.

Willa Cather

How happy are those who can live in your house, always singing your praises. How happy are those who are strong in the Lord....

Psalm 84:4-5 NLT

Honesty

From the time we are children, we are taught that honesty is the best policy, but sometimes, it is so hard to be honest and so easy to be less than honest. So, we convince ourselves that it's alright to tell "little white lies." But there's a problem: Little white lies tend to grow up, and when they do, they cause havoc and pain in our lives. For believers, the issue of honesty is not a topic for debate. Honesty is not just the best policy, it is God's policy, pure and simple. And if we are to be servants worthy of our calling, we will avoid all lies, white or otherwise.

⌐...and put on the new self, which in the likeness of God has been created in righteousness and holiness of the truth. Therefore, laying aside falsehood, speak truth, each one of you, with his neighbor, for we are members of one another.

Ephesians 4:24-25 NASB

Dear Lord, You command Your children to walk in truth. Let me follow Your commandment. Give me the courage to speak honestly, and let me walk righteously with You so that others might see Your eternal truth reflected in my words and my deeds.

Amen

The most exhausting thing in life...is being insincere.

Anne Morrow Lindbergh

It is astonishing what force, purity, and wisdom it requires for a human being to keep clear of falsehoods.

Margaret Fuller

These are the things you are to do: Speak the truth to each other, and render true and sound judgment in your courts....

Zechariah 8:16

Hope

*This world can be a place of trials and tribula-*tions, but as believers we are secure. We need never lose hope because God has promised us peace, joy, and eternal life. So, let us face each day with hope in our hearts and trust in our God. And, let us teach our children to do likewise. After all, God has promised us that we are His throughout eternity, and he keeps His promises. Always.

☞Be of good courage, and he shall strengthen your heart, all ye that hope in the Lord.

Psalm 31:24 KJV

Lord, when my path is steep and my heart is troubled, let me trust in You. When I become discouraged or anxious, let me depend upon You. When I lose faith in this world, let me never lose faith in You. Remind me, Lord, that in every situation and in every season of life, You will love me and protect me. And, with You as my protector, Lord, I need never lose hope because You remain sovereign today and forever.

Amen

To eat bread without hope is still slowly to starve to death.

Pearl Buck

Hope is the feeling you have that the feeling you have isn't permanent.

Jean Kerr

"Hope thou in God." (Psalm 42:5) Oh, remember this: There is never a time when we may not hope in God. Whatever our necessities, however great our difficulties, and though to all appearance help is impossible, yet our business is to hope in God, and it will be found that it is not in vain.

George Muller

*Now the God of hope fill you with
all joy and peace in believing,
that ye may abound in hope.*

Romans 15:13 KJV

Joy

Christ made it clear to His followers that He intended that His joy would become their joy. And it still holds true today: Christ intends that His believers share His love with His joy in their hearts. Yet sometimes, amid the inevitable hustle and bustle of life-here-on-earth, we can forfeit—albeit temporarily—the joy of Christ as we wrestle with the challenges of daily living. Mother Teresa observed, "Joy is the characteristic by which God uses us to re-make the distressing into the desired, the discarded into the creative. Joy is prayer—Joy is strength—Joy is love—Joy is a net of love by which you can catch souls." Joy is God's way; may we seek His joy always.

☞These things have I spoken unto you, that my joy might remain in you, and that your joy might be full.

John 15:11 KJV

Lord, You have created a glorious universe that is far beyond my understanding. You have given me the gift of Your Son. Let me be a joyful Christian, Lord, this day and every day. Today is Your gift to me. Let me use it to Your glory while giving all the praise to You.

Amen

Life really must have joy. It's supposed to be fun!
Barbara Bush

Taking joy in life is a woman's best cosmetic.
Rosalind Russell

Joy is the flag that is flying when the King is on the throne.

Mary Crowley

A child of God should be a visible beatitude for joy and happiness, and a living doxology for gratitude and adoration.

Charles Spurgeon

You will show me the way of life,
granting me the joy of your presence
and the pleasures of living
with you forever.

Psalm 16:11 NLT

87

Judging Others

*W*e have all fallen short of God's commandments, and He has forgiven us. We, too, must forgive others, and we must refrain from judging them. We are warned that to judge others is to invite fearful consequences: to the extent we judge others, so, too, will we be judged by God. Let us resist the temptation of judging our neighbors. Instead, let us forgive them and love them in the same way that God has forgiven us.

☞The LORD does not look at the things man looks at. Man looks at the outward appearance, but the LORD looks at the heart.

1 Samuel 16:7

*L*ord, You know that I can size up others very quickly. And, I can be very wrong. Help me not to judge. I only see a little, but You see the whole. You are the One who searches the heart and knows everything about all of us. You love all Your children, Lord, and so should I.

Amen

We are not placed on this earth to see through each other, but to see each other through.

William M. Kinnaird

An individual Christian may see fit to give up all sorts of things for special reasons—marriage, or meat, or beer, or cinema; but the moment he starts saying the things are bad in themselves, or looking down his nose at other people who do use them, he has taken the wrong turn.

C. S. Lewis

And why beholdest thou the mote that is in thy brother's eye, but considerest not the beam that is in thine own eye?... Thou hypocrite, first cast out the beam out of thine own eye; and then shalt thou see clearly to cast out the mote out of thy brother's eye.

Matthew 7:3,5 KJV

Kindness

If we are to follow the commands of our Lord, we must sow seeds of kindness wherever we go. Kindness is God's way. It should be ours, too. So, today, let's be a little kinder than normal, and let's teach our families and friends the art of kindness through our words and our deeds. People are watching…and so is God.

☞And be ye kind one to another, tenderhearted, forgiving one another, even as God for Christ's sake hath forgiven you.

Ephesians 4:32 KJV

Heavenly Father, sometimes this world can become a demanding place, a place where I rush through the day with my eyes focused only on my next step. Slow me down, Lord, and give me wisdom and peace so that I might look beyond my own needs and see the needs of those around me. Today, help me to be generous, compassionate, and understanding. Today, let me spread kind words and deeds to all who cross my path. And let me show kindness to all who need the healing touch of our Master's hand.

Amen

The nicest thing we can do for our heavenly Father, is to be kind to one of His children.

St. Teresa of Avila

An effort made for the happiness of others lifts us above ourselves.

Lydia M. Child

Kind words can be short and easy to speak, but their echoes are truly endless.

Mother Teresa

While great brilliance and intellect are to be admired, they cannot dry one tear or mend a broken spirit. Only kindness can accomplish this.

John M. Drescher

Verily I say unto you, Inasmuch as ye have done it unto one of the least of these my brethren, ye have done it unto me.

Matthew 25:40 KJV

Knowledge

All of us need both knowledge and wisdom. Knowledge is found in textbooks. Wisdom, on the other hand, is found in God's Holy Word and in the carefully-chosen words of loving and thoughtful teachers. When we give others the gift of knowledge, we do them a wonderful service. But, when we share the gift of wisdom, we offer a timeless treasure that surpasses knowledge and reshapes eternity.

☞The fear of the Lord is the beginning of knowledge, but fools despise wisdom and discipline.

Proverbs 1:7

Teacher...In You is all wisdom and knowledge. Help me to be a student of Your Word and a servant of Your will. May I live by the truth You reveal, and may I teach others the glory of Your ways.

Amen

Your heart often knows things before your mind does.

Polly Adler

Let us remember that the longer we live, the more we know, and the more we know, the more beautiful we are.

Marianne Williamson

We can easily forgive a child who is afraid of the dark; the real tragedy of life is when adults are afraid of the light.

Plato

By wisdom a house is built, and through understanding it is established; through knowledge its rooms are filled with rare and beautiful treasures.

Proverbs 24:3-4

Laughter

It has been said, quite correctly, that laughter is God's medicine. Today, as you go about your daily activities, approach life with a smile and a chuckle. After all, God created laughter for a reason…and Father indeed knows best. So laugh!

☞There is a time for everything, and a season for every activity under heaven…a time to weep and a time to laugh, a time to mourn and a time to dance….

Ecclesiastes 3:1,4

Lord, when I begin to take myself or my life too seriously, let me laugh. When I rush from place to place, slow me down, Lord, and let me laugh. Put a smile on my face, Dear Lord, and let me share that smile with all who cross my path…and let me laugh.

Amen

Laughter dulls the sharpest pain and flattens out the greatest stress. To share it is to give a gift of health....

Barbara Johnson

Laughter is by definition healthy.

Doris Lessing

If you could choose one characteristic that would get you through life, choose a sense of humor.

Jennifer Jones

Laugh and the world laughs with you. Weep and you weep alone.

Ella Wheeler Wilcox

Delicate humor is the crowning virtue of the saints.

Evelyn Underhill

A cheerful heart is good medicine....

Proverbs 17:22

Life

Every day that we awaken, we are confronted with countless opportunities to serve and worship God. When we do, He blesses us. But, when we turn our backs to God, or, when we are simply too busy to acknowledge His greatness, we do ourselves and our families a profound disservice. Life is a glorious opportunity to place ourselves in the service of the One who is the Giver of all blessings. May we seek His will, trust His word, and place Him where He belongs: at the center of our lives.

Now choose life, so that you and your children may live and that you may love the LORD your God, listen to his voice, and hold fast to him. For the LORD is your life, and he will give you many years in the land....

Deuteronomy 30:19-20

You are the Giver of all Life, O Lord, and You created me to have fellowship with You. Let me live a life that pleases You, Lord, and let me thank You always for Your blessings. You love me and protect me, Lord. Let me be grateful, and let me live for You today and throughout eternity.

Amen

We can be victorious but only if we walk with God.

Beth Moore

Life is what we make it. Always has been. Always will be.

Grandma Moses

I will not live my life. I will not spend my life. I will invest my life.

Helen Keller

For whoever finds me finds life and receives favor from the Lord.

Proverbs 8:35

Love

Love is always a choice. Sometimes, of course, we may "fall in love," but it takes work to stay there. Sometimes, we may be "swept off our feet," but the "sweeping" is only temporary; sooner or later, if love is to endure, one must plant one's feet firmly on the ground. The decision to love another person for a lifetime is much more than the simple process of "falling in" or "being swept up." It requires "reaching out," "holding firm," and "lifting up." Love, then, becomes a decision to honor and care for the other person, come what may.

☞As the Father hath loved me, so have I loved you: continue ye in my love. If ye keep my commandments, ye shall abide in my love; even as I have kept my Father's commandments, and abide in his love.

John 15:9-10 KJV

Lord, love is Your commandment. Help me always to remember that the gift of love is a precious gift indeed. Let me nurture love and treasure it. And, keep me mindful that the essence of love is not receiving, it is giving.

Amen

Every circumstance in life, no matter how crooked and distorted and ugly it appears to be, if it is reacted to in love and forgiveness and obedience, can be transformed.

Hannah Hurnard

You always win a better response with love.

Helen Hosier

...only a love that has no regard for vessels and jars—appearances or image—only a love that will lavish its most treasured essence on the feet of Jesus can produce the kind of fragrance that draws cynics and believers alike into His presence.

Gloria Gaither

The story of a love is not important—what is important is that one is capable of love. It is perhaps the only glimpse we are permitted of eternity.

Helen Hayes

But now faith, hope, love, abide these three; but the greatest of these is love.

1 Corinthians 13:13 NASB

Miracles

God is a miracle worker. Throughout history He has intervened in the course of human events in ways which can't be explained by science or human rationale. God's miracles are not limited to Biblical times nor are they witnessed by a select few. Today, God is crafting His wonders all around us: the miracle of the birth of a new baby; the miracle of a world renewing itself with every sunrise; the miracle of lives transformed by God's love and grace. Each day, God's miracles are evident for all to see and experience. May we open our eyes and our hearts to His handiwork.

For with God nothing shall be impossible.

Luke 1:37 KJV

Dear Heavenly Father, Your infinite power is beyond human understanding. With You, Lord, nothing is impossible. Keep me always mindful of Your power, and let me share the glorious message of Your miracles. When I lose hope, give me faith; when others lose hope, let me tell them of Your glory and Your works. Today, Lord, let me expect the miraculous, let me praise You, and let me give thanks for Your miracles.

Amen

I could go through this day oblivious to the miracles all around me or I could tune in and "enjoy."

Gloria Gaither

Where there is great love there are always miracles.

Willa Cather

The invariable mark of wisdom is to see the miraculous in the common.

Ralph Waldo Emerson

Search for the Lord and for his strength, and keep on searching. Think of the wonderful works he has done, the miracles and the judgments he handed down.

Psalm 105:4-5 NLT

Mistakes

The words are all too familiar and all too true: "To err is human...." Yes, we human beings are inclined to make mistakes, and lots of them. When we commit the inevitable blunders of life, let us be quick to correct our errors. And, when we are hurt by the mistakes of others, let us be quick to forgive, just as God has forgiven us.

If we confess our sins, he is faithful and just and will forgive us our sins and purify us from all unrighteousness.

1 John 1:9

Lord, I know that I am imperfect and that I fail You in many ways. Thank You for Your forgiveness and for Your unconditional love. Show me the error of my ways, Lord, that I might confess my wrongdoing and correct my mistakes. And, let me grow each day in wisdom and in faith.

Amen

It is human to err; it is devilish to remain willfully in error.

St. Augustine

There is nothing final about a mistake, except its being taken as final.

Phyllis Bottome

...success is often much harder to deal with than failure. In fact, failure is often good for us human beings; we learn from our failures. We're often destroyed by our success.

Gloria Gaither

He who conceals his sins does not prosper, but whoever confesses and renounces them finds mercy.

Proverbs 28:13

New Beginnings

Each of us, on occasion, experiences the need for renewal and change. Thankfully, our heavenly Father is a God of new beginnings and fresh starts. When we feel defeated or discouraged, we need only turn to God, and He will give us hope. When we feel inadequate, He can give us courage. When we seek to remake ourselves, He can change us in an instant. God is in the business of transforming His children, and when He does, He prepares us for life today and life eternal.

Create in me a pure heart, O God, and renew a steadfast spirit within me.

Psalm 51:10

O Lord, my Creator, conform me to Your image. Create in me a clean heart, a new heart, that reflects the love You lavish on me. Where I need to change, change me, and make me new so that I might follow Your will and praise You always.

Amen

God is not running an antique shop! He is making all things new!

Vance Havner

With God, it's never "Plan B" or "second best." It's always "Plan A." And, if we let Him, He'll make something beautiful of our lives.

Gloria Gaither

Every saint has a past and every sinner has a future.

Anonymous

I will give you a new heart and put a new spirit in you....

Ezekial 36:26

Optimism

*B*elievers have every reason to be optimistic about life. As Corrie ten Boom observed, "If all things are possible with God, then all things are possible to him who believes in him." Today, think optimistically about yourself and your world. And, share your optimism with others. You'll be better for it…and so will they.

☞Finally, brethren, whatsoever things are true, whatsoever things are honest, whatsoever things are just, whatsoever things are pure, whatsoever things are lovely, whatsoever things are of good report; if there be any virtue, and if there be any praise, think on these things.

Philippians 4:8 KJV

*L*ord, help me live expectantly. Let me expect the best from You, and let me look for the best in others. If I become discouraged, Lord, turn my thoughts and my prayers to You. Let me trust You, Lord, to direct my life. And, let me be Your faithful, hopeful, optimistic servant every day that I live.

Amen

The more you praise and celebrate your life, the more there is in life to celebrate.

Oprah Winfrey

An optimist is the human personification of spring.

Susan J. Bissonette

Optimism is that faith that leads to achievement. Nothing can be done without hope and confidence.

Helen Keller

There is wisdom in the habit of looking at the bright side of life.

Father Flanagan

Make me to hear joy and gladness....

Psalm 51:8 KJV

Overcoming Frustration

*A*nger is a natural human emotion that is sometimes necessary and appropriate. When we confront the great evils of this world, we can and should respond with indignation. But, more often than not, our frustrations are of the more mundane variety: checkbooks that won't balance, red lights that won't turn green, children who won't stop crying, and the like. When we are overworked or overwhelmed by the demands of everyday living, anger is both understandable and unfortunate. If we allow ourselves to become angry, we rob ourselves and our loved ones of the peace that God intends for us. A better strategy can be summarized in three simple steps: 1. Forgive early and often 2. Reject perfectionism. 3. Whatever "it" is, let God handle it. He can...and will.

Refrain from anger and turn from wrath; do not fret—it leads only to evil.

Psalm 37:8

*L*ord, I am an imperfect human being; sometimes I am quick to anger and slow to forgive. But, I know that forgiveness is Your commandment, Lord. Let me turn away from anger, and, as I do so, let me claim the peace that You intend for my life.

Amen

To handle yourself, use your head; To handle others, use your heart. Anger is only one letter short of danger.

Eleanor Roosevelt

For every minute you remain angry, you give up sixty seconds of peace of mind.

Ralph Waldo Emerson

When something robs you of your peace of mind, ask yourself if it is worth the energy you are expending on it. If not, then put it out of your mind in an act of discipline. Every time the thought of "it" returns, refuse it.

Kay Arthur

Don't sin by letting anger gain control over you. Think about it overnight....

Psalm 4:4 NLT

Patience

*P*salm 37:7 commands us to wait patiently for God, but, for most of us, waiting quietly for Him is difficult. Why? Because we are fallible human beings, often quick to anger and slow to forgive. Still, God instructs us to be patient in all things, and that's as it should be. After all, think how patient God has been with us.

☞Be still before the Lord and wait patiently for him....

Psalm 37:7

*L*ord, this world can be a demanding place indeed, and I am tempted to rush through my day scarcely giving a thought to the blessings You have given me. There seem to be so many things to accomplish and so little time, Lord, and I am often impatient. Slow me down, Dear Lord, and help me to live on Your timetable, not my own. Keep me mindful that the world is Your creation and that it unfolds according to Your plans. Let me trust Your plans, Lord, with patience and thanksgiving, today and always.

Amen

When I am dealing with an all-powerful, all-knowing God, I, as a mere mortal, must offer my petitions not only with persistence but also with patience. Someday I'll know why.

Ruth Bell Graham

No matter what we are going through, no matter how long the waiting for answers, of one thing we may be sure. God is faithful. He keeps His promises. What he starts, He finishes...including His perfect work in us.

Gloria Gaither

For when the way is rough,
your patience has a chance to grow.
So let it grow, and don't try to squirm
out of your problems.

James 1:3,4 TLB

Peace

The beautiful words of John 14:27 give us hope: "Peace I leave with you, my peace I give unto you...." Jesus offers us peace, not as the world gives, but as He alone gives. We, as believers, can accept His peace or ignore it. When we accept the peace of Christ into our hearts, our lives are transformed. And then, because we possess the gift of peace, we can share that gift with fellow Christians, family members, friends, and associates. May we all claim the inner peace that is our spiritual birthright: the peace of Jesus Christ. It is offered freely; it has been paid for in full: it is ours for the asking. Let us ask. And share.

⟜Blessed are the peacemakers: for they shall be called the children of God.

Matthew 5:9 KJV

Dear God, You offer me a sense of peace that passes all understanding. Let me accept Your peace, Lord, and let me share it with others. And, let me live this day with the assurance of Your love and the power of Your promises, trusting everything to You.

Amen

Peace is full confidence that God is Who He says He is and that he will keep every promise in His Word.

Dorothy Harrison Pentecost

We plant seeds that will flower as results in our lives, so best to remove the weeds of anger, avarice, envy and doubt, that peace and abundance may manifest for all.

Dorothy Day

A great many people are trying to make peace, but that has already been done. God has not left it for us to do; all we have to do is to enter into it.

D. L. Moody

And let the peace of God
rule in your hearts...
and be ye thankful.

Colossians 3:15 KJV

Perfectionism

he difference between perfectionism and ex- cellence is the difference between a life of frustration and a life of satisfaction. Only one being ever lived life to perfection, and He was the Son of God. The rest of us have fallen short of God's standard and need to be accepting of our own limitations as well as the limitations of others. God is perfect; we human beings are not. May we live—and forgive—accordingly.

...for all have sinned, and come short of the glory of God....

Romans 3:23 KJV

hank you Lord, for the perfect example of how to live: Your Son, Jesus Christ. Help me always to strive to do my best and to confess my sins when I fall short. And, when others fall short, let me forgive them, Lord, just as You have forgiven me.

Amen

Excellence is not perfection, but essentially a desire to be strong in the Lord and for the Lord.

Cynthia Heald

Striving for excellence motivates you; striving for perfection is demoralizing.

Dr. Harriet Braiker

Striving for perfection is the greatest stopper there is....It's your excuse to yourself for not doing anything. Instead, strive for excellence, doing your best.

Sir Laurence Olivier

Whatever your hand finds to do, do it with all your might....

Ecclesiastes 9:10

Perseverance

The old saying is as true today as it was when it was first spoken: "Life is a marathon, not a sprint." Life, indeed, requires perseverance, so wise travelers select a traveling companion who never tires and never falters. That partner, of course, is God. Are you tired? Ask God for strength. Are you discouraged? Believe in His promises. Are you defeated? Pray as if everything depended upon God, and work as if everything depended upon yourself. With God's help, you can persevere…and you will.

⌐Let us not become weary in doing good, for at the proper time we will reap a harvest if we do not give up.

Galatians 6:9

Lord, sometimes, this life is difficult indeed. Sometimes, we are burdened or fearful. Sometimes, we cry tears of bitterness or loss, but even then, You never leave our sides. Today, Lord, let me be a finisher of my faith. Let me persevere— even if the day is difficult—and let me follow Your Son Jesus Christ this day and forever.

Amen

There is no chance, no destiny, no fate, that can hinder or control the firm resolve of a determined soul.

Ella Wheeler Wilcox

When you get into a tight place and everything goes against you, till it seems as though you could not hang on a minute longer, never give up then, for that is just the place and the time the tide will turn.

Harriet Beecher Stowe

You may have to fight a battle more than once to win it.

Margaret Thatcher

...let us throw off everything that hinders and the sin that so easily entangles, and let us run with perseverance the race marked out for us.

Hebrews 12:1

117

Possessions

On the grand stage of a well-lived life, material possessions should play a rather small role. Of course, we all need the basic necessities of life, but once we meet those needs for ourselves and for our families, the piling up of possessions creates more problems than it solves. Our real riches, of course, are not of this world. We are never really rich until we are rich in spirit.

Lay not up for yourselves treasures upon earth, where moth and rust doth corrupt, and where thieves break through and steal: but lay up for yourselves treasures in heaven...for where your treasure is, there will your heart be also.

Matthew 6:19-21 KJV

*Lord... my greatest possession is my relation*ship with You. You have promised that, when I first seek Your kingdom and Your righteousness, You will give me whatever I need. Let me trust You completely, Lord, for my needs, both material and spiritual, this day and always.

Amen

He is no fool who gives what he cannot keep to gain what he cannot lose.

Jim Elliot

Prosperity depends more on wanting what you have than having what you want.

Geoffrey F. Abert

...a man's life does not consist in the abundance of his possessions.

Luke 12:15

Praise

It has been called the most widely-used book of the Old Testament; it is, of course, the book of Psalms. In the Hebrew version of the Old Testament, the title of the book is translated "hymns of praise," and with good reason. Much of the book is a breathtakingly beautiful celebration of God's power, God's love, and God's creation. The psalmist writes, "Let everything that has breath praise the Lord. Praise the Lord." (150:6) We should continually praise God for all that He has done and all that He will do. For believers, there is simply no other way. Today, may we praise the Giver of all things good for His marvelous works. His gifts are beyond understanding, and His love endures forever.

From the rising of the sun to its setting, the name of the LORD is to be praised.

Psalm 113:3 NASB

Lord, Your hand created the smallest grain of sand and the grandest stars in the heavens. You watch over Your entire creation, and You watch over me. Heavenly Father, Your gifts are greater than I can imagine, and Your love for me is greater than I can fathom. May I live each day with thanksgiving in my heart and praise on my lips.

Amen

Preoccupy my thoughts with your praise beginning today.

Joni Eareckson Tada

Praise—lifting up our heart and hands, exulting with our voices, singing his praises—is the occupation of those who dwell in the kingdom.

Max Lucado

Sing praises to God, sing praises: sing praises unto our King, sing praises. For God is the King of all the earth: sing ye praises with understanding.

Psalm 47:6-7 KJV

Prayer

*P*rayer changes things and it changes us.
Today, instead of turning things over
in your mind, turn them over to God in prayer. Instead of worrying about your next decision, ask God to lead the way. Don't limit your prayers to meals or to bedtime. Pray constantly about things great and small. God is listening, and He wants to hear from you.

Rejoice evermore. Pray without ceasing. In every thing give thanks: for this is the will of God in Christ Jesus concerning you.

1 Thessalonians 5:16-18 KJV

*D*ear Lord, Your Holy Word commands me
to pray without ceasing. Let me take everything to You in prayer. When I am discouraged, let me pray. When I am lonely, let me take my sorrows to You. When I grieve, let me take my tears to You, Lord, in prayer. And when I am joyful, let me offer up prayers of thanksgiving. In all things great and small, at all times, whether happy or sad, let me seek Your wisdom and Your Grace…in prayer.

Amen

When we pray, it is far more important to pray with a sense of the greatness of God than with a sense of the greatness of the problem.

Evangeline Blood

A demanding spirit, with self-will as its rudder, blocks prayer….Prayer is men cooperating with God in bringing from heaven to earth His wondrously good plans for us.

Catherine Marshall

Is prayer your steering wheel or your spare tire?

Corrie ten Boom

For the eyes of the Lord are over the righteous, and his ears are open unto their prayers….

I Peter 3:12 KJV

123

Renewal

God intends that His children lead joyous lives filled with abundance and peace. But sometimes, as all women can attest, abundance and peace seem very far away. It is then that we must turn to God for renewal, and when we do, He will restore us. Are you tired or troubled? Turn your heart toward God in prayer. Are you weak or worried? Make the time to delve deeply into God's Holy Word. When you do, you'll discover that the Creator of the universe stands ready and able to create a new sense of wonderment and joy in you.

He restoreth my soul.

Psalm 23:3 KJV

Heavenly Father, sometimes I am troubled, and sometimes I grow weary. When I am weak, Lord, give me strength. When I am discouraged, renew me. When I am fearful, let me feel Your healing touch. Let me always trust in Your promises, Lord, and let me draw strength from those promises and from Your unending love.

Amen

The amazing thing about Jesus is that He doesn't just patch up our lives….He gives us a brand new sheet, a clean slate to start over, all new.

Gloria Gaither

I wish I could make it all new again…I can't. But God can. "He restores my soul," wrote the shepherd. He doesn't reform; he restores. He doesn't camouflage the old; he restores the new. The Master Builder will pull out the original plan and restore it. He will restore the vigor, he will restore the energy. He will restore the hope. He will restore the soul.

Max Lucado

What we call the beginning is often the end. And to make an end is to make a beginning. The end is where we start from.

T. S. Eliot

Remember ye not the former things, neither consider the things of old. Behold, I will do a new thing….

Isaiah 43:18,19 KJV

Seeking God

Where is God? He is everywhere you have ever been and everywhere you will ever go. He is with you night and day; He knows your every thought; He hears every heartbeat. When you earnestly seek Him, you will find Him because He is here, waiting patiently for you to reach out to Him…right here.

☞The LORD is good to those whose hope is in him, to the one who seeks Him….

Lamentations 3:25

How comforting it is, Dear Lord, to know that if I seek You, I will find You. You are with me, Lord, every step I take. Let me reach out to You, and let me praise You for revealing Your Word, Your way, and Your love.

Amen

You must always work at practicing God's presence. Not to advance in the spiritual life is to go backward.... We should establish ourselves in a sense of God's presence by continually conversing with Him.

Brother Lawrence

As God perfects us, He keeps us protected from the pride that might otherwise develop by veiling to some extent our progress in our own eyes....The light of the glory of His presence shines two ways: it sheds light on the knowledge of God so that we can learn to see Him more clearly, but it also sheds light on us so that we can see our own sin more clearly.

Beth Moore

Be strong and courageous.
Do not be terrified; do not be
discouraged, for the Lord your God
will be with you wherever you go.

Joshua 1:9

Self-acceptance

*F*aith in God leads to self-acceptance. Without God, a woman may be plagued with doubts about self-worth and self-esteem. But, the believer knows that God created her in His image and that she was recreated by her belief in God's Son. The Bible affirms the importance of self-acceptance when exhorting believers to love others as they love themselves. When we turn our hearts to Him, God accepts us just as we are. And, if He accepts us—faults and all—then who are we to believe otherwise?

☞For you made us only a little lower than God, and you crowned us with glory and honor.

Psalm 8:5 NLT

*H*eavenly Father, keep me ever-mindful that I am created in Your image. I am a child of the King. I have been adopted and accepted into the family of God. Help me to live in a way that is worthy of the position You have given me, and let me follow Your Word and Your will for my life today and every day.

Amen

When one is estranged from oneself, then one is estranged from others, too.

Anne Morrow Lindbergh

Look for the good in everybody, starting with yourself.

Marie T. Freeman

You are God's chief creation, and you are here for His pleasure and His glory.

Beth Moore

... He [God] who began a good work in you will carry it on to completion....

Philippians 1:6

Serving Others

*J*esus teaches that the most esteemed men and women are not the self-congratulatory leaders of society but are instead the humblest of servants. Today, you may feel the temptation to build yourself up in the eyes of your neighbors. Resist that temptation. Instead, serve your neighbors quietly and without fanfare. Find a need and fill it...humbly. Lend a helping hand and share a word of kindness...anonymously. This is God's way.

☞Each of you should look not only to your own interests, but also to the interest of others.

Philippians 2:4

*F*ather in heaven...when Jesus humbled Himself and became a servant, He also became an example for His followers. Today, as I serve my family and friends, I do so in obedience to the example set by Jesus Christ. May I do so willingly, humbly, and prayerfully.

Amen

Christians are like the several flowers in a garden that have each of them the dew of heaven, which, being shaken by the wind, they let fall at each other's roots, whereby they are jointly nourished, and become nourishers of each other.

John Bunyan

We can't help everyone, but everyone can help someone.

Loretta Scott

If you're too busy to give your neighbor a helping hand, then you're just too busy.

Marie T. Freeman

Be devoted to one another in brotherly love. Honor one another above yourselves.

Romans 12:10

Sharing

We live in a fast-paced, competitive world where it is easy to say, "Me first." But, God instructs us to do otherwise. In God's kingdom, those who proclaim, "Me first," are last. God loves a cheerful, selfless giver. If we seek greatness in God's eyes, we must look our neighbors squarely in the eye and say, "You first." When we do, we will set an example for others in how God wants all His children to live.

☞…so let him give; not grudgingly, or of necessity: for God loveth a cheerful giver.

II Corinthians 9:7 KJV

Lord, I know there is no happiness in keeping Your blessings for myself. True joy is found in sharing what I have with others. Make me a generous, loving, humble servant, Dear Lord, that my joy may be full.

Amen

People don't care how much you know until they know how much you care.

John Maxwell

The nicest thing we can do for our heavenly Father, is to be kind to one of His children.

St. Teresa of Avila

When you extend hospitality to others, you're not trying to impress people, you're trying to reflect God to them.

Max Lucado

In everything I did, I showed you that by this kind of hard work we must help the weak, remembering the words the Lord Jesus himself said: 'It is more blessed to give than to receive.'

Acts 20:35

Strength

*G*od is a never-ending source of strength and courage for those who call upon Him. When we are weary, He gives us strength. When we see no hope, God reminds us of His promises. When we grieve, God wipes away our tears. Whatever our circumstances, God will protect us and care for us…if we let Him.

☞I can do all things through Him who strengthens me.

Philippians 4:13 NASB

*L*ord, sometimes life is difficult. Sometimes, I am worried, weary, or heartbroken. But, when I lift my eyes to You, Lord, You strengthen me. When I am weak, You lift me up. Today, let me turn to You, Lord, for my strength and my salvation.

Amen

He goes before us, follows behind us, and hems us safe inside the realm of His protection.

Beth Moore

God gives us always strength enough, and sense enough, for every thing he wants us to do.

John Ruskin

Cast your cares on God; that anchor holds.

Alfred, Lord Tennyson

The Lord is the strength of my life.

Psalm 27:1 KJV

Temptation

How hard is it to bump into temptation in this crazy world? Not very hard. The devil, it seems, is working overtime these days, and causing pain and heartache in more places and in more ways than ever before. We must remain vigilant. Not only must we resist Satan when he confronts us, but we must also avoid those places where Satan can most easily tempt us. We must beware, and we must earnestly wrap ourselves in the protection of God's Holy Word. When we do, we are secure.

⌒There hath no temptation taken you but such as is common to man: but God is faithful, who will not suffer you to be tempted above that ye are able; but will with the temptation also make a way to escape, that ye may be able to bear it.

I Corinthians 10:13 KJV

Lord, this world is filled with temptations, distractions, and frustrations. When I turn my thoughts away from You and Your Word, Lord, I suffer. But when I trust in Your commandments, I am safe. Direct my path far from the temptations and distractions of the world. Let me discover Your will and follow it, Dear Lord, this day and always.

Amen

Jesus faced every temptation known to humanity so that He could identify with us.

Beth Moore

You have to say "yes" to God first before you can effectively say "no" to the devil.

Vance Havner

Because Christ has faced our every temptation without sin, we never face a temptation that has no door of escape.

Beth Moore

... be vigilant; because your adversary the devil, as a roaring lion, walketh about, seeking whom he may devour.

I Peter 5:8 KJV

Today

The 118th Psalm reminds us that today, like every other day, is a cause for celebration. God gives us this day; He fills it to the brim with possibilities, and He challenges us to use it to His purposes. The day is presented to us fresh and clean at midnight, free of charge, but we must beware: Today is a non-renewable resource—once it's gone, it's gone forever. Our responsibility, of course, is to use this day in the service of God's will and according to His commandments.

☞This is the day the Lord has made; let us rejoice and be glad in it.

Psalm 118:24

Help me, Father, to learn from the past but not live in it. And, help me to plan for the future but not to worry about it. This is the day You have given me, Lord. Let me use it according to Your master plan, and let me give thanks for Your blessings. Enable me to live each moment to the fullest, totally involved in Your will.

Amen

138

The past, the present and the future are really one. They are today.

Harriet Beecher Stowe

Make each day useful and cheerful and prove that you know the worth of time by employing it well. Then youth will be happy, old age without regret, and life a beautiful success.

Louisa May Alcott

Give your entire attention to what God is doing right now, and don't get worked up about what may or may not happen tomorrow. God will help you deal with whatever hard things come up when the time comes.

Matthew 6:33,34 MSG

139

Trust in God

*D*o you aspire to do great things for God's kingdom? Then trust Him. Trust Him with every aspect of your life. Trust Him with your relationships. Follow His commandments and pray for His guidance. Then, wait patiently for God's revelations and for His blessings. In His own fashion and in His own time, God will bless you in ways that you never could have imagined.

Trust in the LORD with all thine heart; and lean not unto thine own understanding. In all thy ways acknowledge him, and he shall direct thy paths.

Proverbs 3:5-6 KJV

*L*ord, when I trust in things of this earth, I will be disappointed. But when I put my faith in You, I am secure. You are my rock and my shield. Upon Your firm foundation I will build my life. When I am worried, Lord, let me trust in You. You will love me and protect me, and You will share Your boundless grace today, tomorrow, and forever.

Amen

When we trust the author; we don't have to know the story. We just know it will be true.

Gloria Gaither

Either we are adrift in chaos or we are individuals, created, loved, upheld and placed purposefully, exactly where we are. Can you believe that? Can you trust God for that?

Elisabeth Elliot

When we are in a situation where Jesus is all we have, we soon discover he is all we really need.

Gigi Graham Tchividjian

In thee, O Lord, do I put my trust....

Psalm 31:1 KJV

Truth

The words of John 8:32 are both familiar and profound: "Ye shall know the truth, and the truth shall make you free." Truth is God's way: He commands His children to live in truth, and He rewards those who follow his commandment. Jesus is the personification of a perfect, liberating truth that offers salvation to mankind. Do you seek to walk with God? Then you must walk in truth.

☞ ...as we have received mercy, we faint not; but have renounced the hidden things of dishonesty, not walking in craftiness, nor handling the word of God deceitfully; but, by manifestation of the truth, commending ourselves to every man's conscience in the sight of God.

II Corinthians 4:1-2 KJV

Heavenly Father, you are the way and the truth and the light. Today, as I follow Your way, and live in Your truth, and share Your light with others, I thank You for the inevitable result in my life—freedom.

Amen

Those who walk in truth walk in liberty.

Beth Moore

Truth is the only safe ground to stand upon.

Elizabeth Cady Stanton

One with God is a majority.

Billy Graham

But when he, the Spirit of truth, comes, he will guide you into all truth....

John 16:13

Work

It has been said that there are no shortcuts to anyplace worth going. Hard work is not simply a proven way to get ahead, it's also part of God's plan for His children. God did not create us for lives of mediocrity; He created us for far greater things. Earning great things usually requires work and lots of it, which is perfectly fine with God. After all, He knows that we're up to the task, and He has big plans for us. Very big plans…

☞But as for you, be strong and do not give up, for your work will be rewarded.

II Chronicles 15:7

Lord, I know that You desire a bountiful harvest for all Your children. But, You have instructed us that we must sow before we reap, not after. Help me, Lord, to sow the seeds of Your abundance everywhere I go. Let me be diligent in all my undertakings and give me patience to wait for Your harvest. In time, Lord, let me reap the harvest that is found in Your will for my life.

Amen

Ordinary work, which is what most of us do most of the time, is ordained by God every bit as much as is the extraordinary.

Elisabeth Elliot

I seem to have been led little by little, toward my work; and I believe that the same fact will appear in the life of anyone who will cultivate such powers as God has given him, and then go on, bravely, quietly, but persistently, doing such work as comes to his hands.

Fanny Crosby

I long to accomplish a great and noble task, but it is my chief duty to accomplish small tasks as if they were great and noble.

Helen Keller

Work hard so God can say to you, "Well done." Be a good workman, one who does not need to be ashamed when God examines your work....

2 Timothy 2:15 TLB

145

Worry

All of us, from time to time, worry about the inevitable challenges of everyday life. We worry about finances, about safety, about education, and about countless other issues, some great and some small. Where is the best place to take our worries? We should take them to God. When we do, He blesses us and protects us. May we all seek protection from the One who can never be moved.

⟶Yea, though I walk through the valley of the shadow of death, I will fear no evil: for thou art with me; thy rod and thy staff they comfort me.

Psalm 23:4 KJV

Forgive me, Lord, when I worry. Worry re- flects a lack of trust in Your ability to meet my every need. Help me to work, Lord, and not to worry. And, keep me mindful, Lord, that nothing, absolutely nothing, will happen this day that You and I cannot handle together.

Amen

He manages perfectly, day and night, year in and year out, the movements of the stars, the wheeling of the planets, the staggering coordination of events that goes on at the molecular level in order to hold things together. There is no doubt that he can manage the timing of my days and weeks.

Elisabeth Elliot

Submit each day to God, knowing that He is God over all your tomorrows.

Kay Arthur

So do not worry, saying 'What shall we eat' or 'What shall we drink?' or 'What shall we wear?' But seek first his kingdom and his righteousness, and all these things will be given to you as well. Therefore do not worry about tomorrow, for tomorrow will worry about itself. Each day has enough trouble of its own.

Matthew 6:31,33,34

Worship

When we worship God, either alone or in the company of fellow believers, we are blessed. When we fail to worship God, for whatever reason, we forfeit the spiritual riches that are rightfully ours. Every day provides opportunities to put God where He belongs: at the center of our lives. Let us worship Him, and only Him, today and always.

⌐Happy are those who hear the joyful call to worship, for they will walk in the light of your presence, Lord.

Psalm 89:15 NLT

In the quiet moments, before the day begins to unfold with all its clamor and distractions, let me worship You, Almighty God. And, throughout this day, let me give You thanks and praise for Your marvelous gifts. May my worship bring You pleasure, and may the time I spend in devotion to You mold me into the person You desire me to be.

Amen

In Biblical worship you do not find the repetition of a phrase; instead, you find the worshipers rehearsing the character of God and His ways, reminding Him of His faithfulness and His wonderful promises.

Kay Arthur

Worship and worry cannot live in the same heart: they are mutually exclusive.

Ruth Graham

If you will not worship God seven days a week, you do not worship Him on one day a week.

A. W. Tozer

All the earth shall worship thee,
and shall sing unto thee;
and shall sing to thy name....

Psalm 66:4 KJV